TRADE & WARFARE

ROBERT HULL

FRANKLIN WATTS

NEW YORK • LONDON • SYDNEY

First published in 1999
by Franklin Watts, 96 Leonard Street,
London EC2A 4XD

Franklin Watts Australia
14 Mars Road, Lane Cove
NSW 2066

Series editor: Rachel Cooke
Designer: White Design
Consultant: Dr Anne Millard
Picture research: Susan Mennell
Artwork: Peter Bull Art Studio

A CIP catalogue record for this book
is available from the British Library.

ISBN 0 7496 3296 8

Dewey Classification 938

Printed in Dubai U.A.E.

Acknowledgements: AKG London cover l (Louvre, Paris/
E. Lessing), tr (Staatl. Antikenslg. & Glyptothek., Munich), br
(Louvre, Paris/E. Lessing), pp. 2-3 (E. Lessing), 4t (National
Archeological Museum, Athens), 5t (Haaretz Museum, Tel
Aviv), 5b (Israel Museum (IDAM), Jerusalem/E. Lessing), 6b
(National Maritime Museum, Haifa/E. Lessing), 7t
(E. Lessing), 7b (National Archeological Museum, Beirut/
E. Lessing), 8 (Staatl. Antikenslg. & Glyptothek., Munich),
12t (Delphi Museum/E. Lessing), 13bl (E. Lessing), 14t
(Akademie den Bildenden Kuenste/E. Lessing), 15t (Louvre,
Paris/E. Lessing), 15cr (National Archeological Museum,
Athens/E. Lessing), 15b (British Museum/E. Lessing), 16t
(E. Lessing), 16b (Louvre, Paris/E. Lessing), 17t (Louvre,
Paris), 19t (British Museum/E. Lessing), 20b (Louvre, Paris/
E. Lessing), 21 (SMPK, Antidenmuseum, Berlin), 22 (Louvre,
Paris/E. Lessing), 24t (Louvre, Paris/E. Lessing), 24b
(E. Lessing), 25 (Musée Vivenel, Compiegne), 26r (Pergamon
Museum), 26l (E. Lessing), 27r (Museé Vivenel, Compiegne/
E. Lessing), 28t (Bibliotheque Nationale, Paris), 28b
(National Museum of Archeology, Naples), 29 (Archeological
Museum, Istanbul/E. Lessing);
Ancient Art and Architecture Collection pp. 11b (Brian
Wilson), 12b (Ronald Sheridan), 19b (Ronald Sheridan);
Automobile Association Photo Library pp. 15cl, 18r; e.t.
Archive pp. 6t (National Museum, Athens), 13tr (Louvre,
Paris), 14b (Acropolis Museum, Athens), 18l (Acheological
Museum, Ferrara), 20t (Archeological Museum, Salonica);
Robert Harding Picture Library p. 10; John Heseltine p. 11t;
Robert Hull p. 13tl; Hulton Getty Collection p. 27l;
Hutchison Picture Library p. 17b (Nick Haslam);
Travel Ink pp. 9l (Nigel Bowen-Morris), 9r (Rawdon Wyatt).

CONTENTS

EARLY TRADE

With a long coastline and many islands, the ancient Greeks were always going to be travellers. They sailed long distances to exchange goods peacefully, or to raid and plunder. They travelled to find new homes, and they spread Greek ideas through the ancient world.

A 13th-century BC fresco from the island of Thera (Santorini) showing Minoan boats leaving port.

Ancient sea traders

As early as about 8000 BC, Greeks were criss-crossing the Aegean Sea to mine rock or flint on various islands. By about 3000 BC, Greek metal workers were making bronze, using copper from Cyprus and Sardinia, and tin from the east and the west.

gold
seal stones
copper
ITALY
SARDINIA
tin
SICILY
GREECE
ivory, tin
CYPRUS
CRETE
copper
CANAAN
MEDITERRANEAN SEA
copper
ostrich eggs
gold, ivory
EGYPT

UNDER MYCENAEAN CONTROL
EXPORTS (mainly pottery & olive oil)
IMPORTS

Under the Minoans, Crete was the first great centre of trade. Their ships carried olive oil and other goods south to Egypt and all around the eastern Mediterranean. There are written records, on clay tablets, of their trade and their local taxes.

This map shows early Minoan and Mycenaean trade links.

The Mycenaeans

From about 1500 BC, Mycenaeans from mainland Greece took over from the Minoans as the main traders in the area. Mycenaean kings exchanged gifts peacefully with Egyptian pharaohs. The Greeks took olive oil, wine and pottery, and, in return, received alabaster, gold, ivory and ostrich eggs.

Other Mycenaean merchants went to Babylon, Thrace and the Black Sea. Bits of their pottery have been found in Libya, Israel, Sardinia and even Italy.

archaeologist: Our modern word means someone who studies the remains of the past. It comes from two Greek words: *archai* – the beginning – and *logos* – words.

A bronze necklace made in Mycenae between 1550 and 1200 BC. It was found in modern Israel.

THEIR OWN WORDS

In this letter a Cypriot king of about 1300 BC orders goods from the king of Egypt.

'A message from the King of Cyprus to the King of Egypt. My brother, I send a messenger to you with 100 talents of copper. Will your messenger please bring me one ebony bed trimmed with gold, one chariot with two horses, fourteen beams of ebony, and some bales of the finest linen.'

A 'Dark Age' begins

But around 1250 BC, the early Greek cities were burnt and destroyed. Famine may have caused Greeks from the islands or the colonies of what is now Turkey to attack the mainland. Over the next 150 years the cities disappeared, writing was forgotten, and the Greeks no longer travelled as they had done. A 'Dark Age' began.

This Mycenaean goblet was exported from mainland Greece to Canaan (modern Israel).

AFTER the DARK AGE

During the Dark Age, there was hardly any new building in stone or brick, and not much artistic craft work. Greeks travelled and traded much less and had much less contact with the rest of the world.

Reviving Greece

City life continued in Athens and at places like Lefkandi on the island of Euboea. Pottery was still made in many towns. The Greeks kept up some trade, especially with Cyprus, where iron objects like knives and axes were made. These hard new iron axes cut down trees more quickly than bronze axes, so ships could be built more easily.

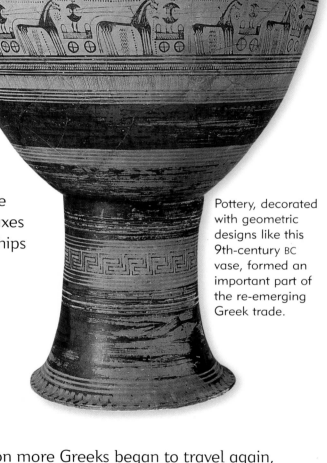

Pottery, decorated with geometric designs like this 9th-century BC vase, formed an important part of the re-emerging Greek trade.

From the 8th century BC, the Greek city of Corinth exported vases like this, in ships like those painted on its side.

Soon more Greeks began to travel again, searching for metals like tin and copper, selling pottery and exploring. Communities grew larger. From about 800 BC, the Greeks combined cities and their surrounding farmland into 'city-states'. With busy city-states came more travel and trade.

Competition

During the Dark Age, the Phoenicians, the Canaanite people who lived along the coast of modern Lebanon, had taken over from the Mycenaean Greeks as the main traders in the area.

But Greek traders began to rival them again. They settled at Al Mina in Syria, sending wine and oil by river and overland to Babylon, and taking home fine fabrics, ivory, gold, tin and slaves — just as the Mycenaeans had done. They set up trading centres at Naucratis in Egypt, and Cyrene in north Africa.

LEGACY

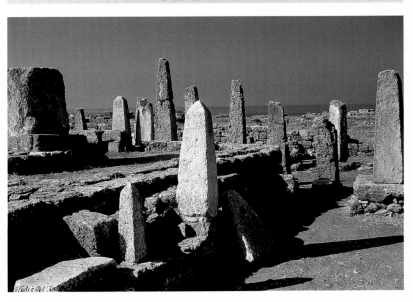

The remains of a Phoenician temple at Byblos, in modern Lebanon.

This Phoenician silver coin shows a ship and hippocamp (a type of sea-monster).

During the Dark Age, the Mycenaean way of writing and keeping records had been forgotten. But new ideas are carried by trade and travel. When some Phoenicians came to Greece, says Herodotus, 'They brought the alphabet, which … had not been known to the Greeks… The Greeks who lived amongst the Phoenicians learned the alphabet from them, making a few changes in the form of the letters…' The Romans in turn adapted the Greek alphabet and this became our own.

Plunder or fair exchange

Some trade was really plunder, stolen by acts of piracy or in minor skirmishes. Most trade was barter — peacefully swopping things, perhaps on the beach. Merchants from Babylon and beyond laid out their precious goods, and took the Greeks' specialities in exchange.

SHIPS AND SEA TRAVEL

To the Greeks, ships and sailing were vital. Without ships, the Greeks could not move from island to island for trade, travel or warfare. Themistokles, a famous leader, said, 'So long as we have our ships, we Athenians have a city.'

anchor: Our word 'anchor' is almost the same as the Greek word *ankura*.

Ships

From early times, ships were built of oak, fir or poplar, with a supple mast of fir. They were crescent-shaped, with a tall stern. Warships were narrow for speed and had rowers as well as a mast; merchant ships were wider and relied on sails and a steering oar. The ships were anchored with large stones.

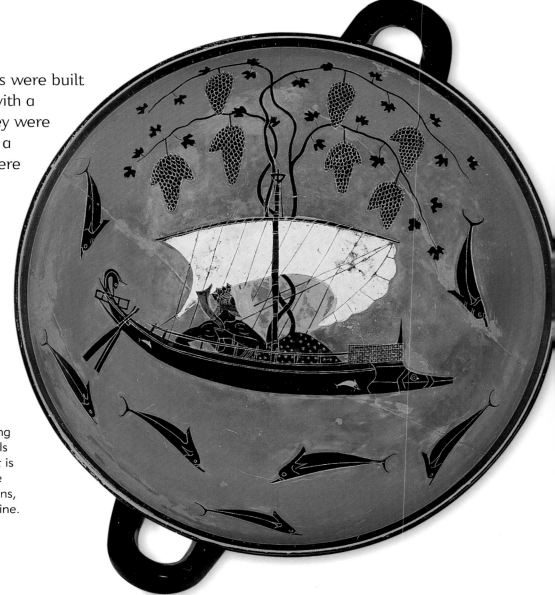

In this 6th-century BC drinking cup, the god Dionysus travels in a Greek merchant ship. It is attacked by pirates, who are magically turned into dolphins, while the mast becomes a vine.

The weather

Ships only sailed when the weather was good, between late spring and early autumn. Even then, sailing could be dangerous. Storms blew up, and there was no compass or sextant for navigation, only the sun and stars, and landmarks. So most Greek ships, which were small and slow anyway and couldn't sail against headwinds, stayed close to land, carrying goods locally from one harbour to the next.

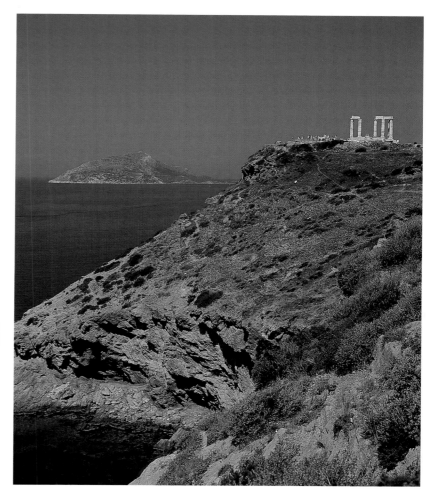

The broken, rocky coastline of Greece was hard to navigate. At the top of this headland, Cape Souniun, is a temple to Poseidon, god of the sea. Greek sailors would pray to him for a safe journey.

■■■LEGACY■■■

Sea-travel is as much a part of modern Greece as it was 2000 years ago. At harbours like Piraeus (pictured above) and Patras you can see ships from every corner of the Mediterranean, just as in ancient times. From all over Europe, lorries, coaches and cars arrive in Patras on the big Greek ferries from Italy. Cars and lorries travel to the islands by boat, and so does most traffic between north and south Greece.

Travelling overland

Overland transport was expensive and difficult in a land of mountains and rough tracks. Mule-teams and ox-carts were slow but merchants did go overland when they had to. Journeys west from Athens often avoided going round the southern tip of the Peloponnese; instead, merchants hauled boats overland along a stone track – a *diolchos* – across the thin land-bridge which joined the Peloponnese to the rest of Greece.

GREEK COLONIES

Between about 800 and 500 BC, many Greeks sailed away to new homes. They went west to Italy and Sicily, south to Africa, and north to Thrace and Macedonia and the Black Sea.

EUROPE

GAUL

SCYTHIA

Massalia

BLACK SEA

Saguntum

Sinope

IBERIA

Taras

Croton Sparta Athens Miletus

Syracuse

PHOENICIA

Cyrene

Naucratis

EGYPT

■ COLONIES

→ Ionian speakers
→ Doric speakers
(principal Greek dialects)

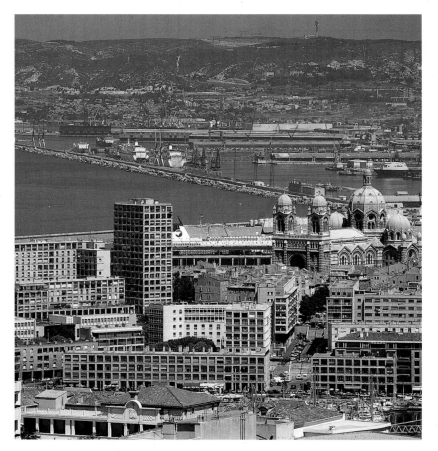

Invading colonists

The Greeks went for many reasons – quarrels in the city, overcrowding due to a rapid population growth, famine and greed. Many settlements were like invasions. In Sicily, Greek colonists drove out the local Sicel people to found Naxos, then built thick walls for protection.

Colonists were often looking for slaves or precious metals. In 600 BC, the Phocians from central Greece founded Massalia (modern Marseilles), took control of the tin trade with Britain and sent slaves to Greece from the local tribes.

Modern Marseilles, originally the Greek colony Massalia, and still one of the busiest ports in the Mediterranean.

'Great Greece'

Many Greeks settled in Sicily and southern Italy – *Magna Graecia* or 'Great Greece'. The area became very prosperous as it had rich agricultural land and could sell much cheese and pork to Greece. Syracuse became the biggest city in the Greek world.

THEIR OWN WORDS

One later Roman writer, Justinus, thought that the coming of the Greek colonists was a very good thing for the people of Gaul (in this case, France and Spain):

'From the Greeks the Gauls learned a more civilized way of life... They began tilling their fields and walling their towns. They began to live according to the law, and grow vines and olives... It seemed they had become part of Greece, not that Greece had colonized Gaul.'

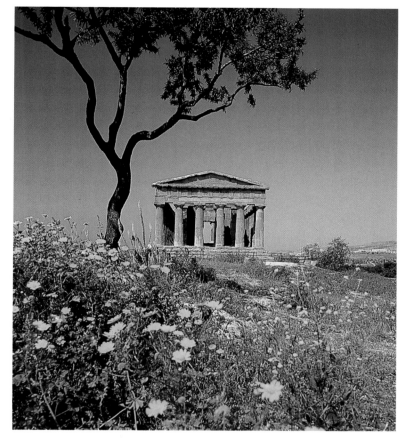

The Greeks built temples in their colonies. This is the Temple of Concord at Agrigento on Sicily.

Greek colonies often minted their own coins. This one from Tarentum in Italy shows its founder, Taras, arriving on a dolphin.

Trade and conflict

New settlements kept up close links with the mother-cities; and when colonies sent out their own colonists, the founder had to be from the mother-city too. Trading was an important part of the link. When colonists from Miletus founded cities on the coasts of the Black Sea, Milesian goods were exported there, in return for local products.

Alongside the trade was plenty of fighting. In Sicily the Greeks fought the Carthaginians. Greek fought Greek, too. In 520 BC, the Italian Greek city of Croton destoyed a wealthy neighbouring city, Sybaris.

PIRATES AND PLUNDER

On their expeditions the early Greeks might barter wine and oil for things like copper and tin. But they might also raid, kidnap and plunder to get what they wanted. Trade, war, plunder and piracy were often closely linked; one could easily turn into the other.

pirate: We get our word pirate from the Greek word *peirates*, meaning a sea-robber.

Piracy or war?

It was sometimes hard to tell the difference between war and piracy. Homer's noble hero, Odysseus, sometimes behaves like a pirate. He attacks a people called the Kikones, kills the men and makes slaves of the women. He also pretends to have been a well-known Cretan pirate.

Piracy was a weapon of war, too. In one war the Athenians carried out acts of piracy and plunder against their enemy, who had previously kidnapped Athenian merchants. Athenian ships seized fishing-boats and ships carrying corn.

Gold and ivory, such as made this head, were the sort of rich cargoes that attracted pirates.

A pirate attack? A heavy grain ship is about to be rammed by a light-weight warship.

The pirate problem

Pirates were always a problem for Greek traders, especially in the west, but also in the north near Thrace, and in the Black Sea. There were treaties — legal arrangements — between cities to try to stamp it out. In the 4th century BC, Philip of Macedon, who became the conqueror of all Greece, quarrelled with the Athenians because they were not doing enough to clear the seas of pirates.

The narrow streets that lead to many Greek harbours were originally a defence against pirates.

But piracy couldn't be rooted out. The pirates had too many bases in the Greek world, and pirate plunder made some cities prosperous, especially those that relied on the slave trade. The island of Aegina, for instance, had few riches of its own but grew very prosperous through piracy.

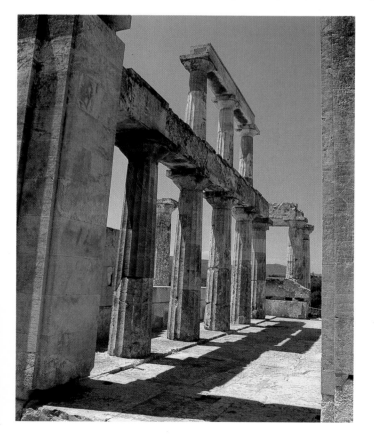

A bronze statuette of an African slave, perhaps captured in a Greek raid (right).

Money from piracy helped build the temple of Athena on Aegina (left).

THEIR OWN WORDS

When Alexander the Great captured a pirate and threatened to put him to death, the pirate defended himself by saying: *'Because I raid with a small boat I'm called a pirate. You do the same thing with a large army and you're called an emperor.'*

13

TRADE INSIDE GREECE

As the cities of Greece grew bigger and richer, they began to trade more. Even wars didn't stop trade; Greek wars were not continuous, and brief battles interfered no longer than bouts of bad weather.

A 6th-century BC vase painting of traders carrying and weighing cloth.

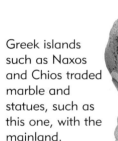

Greek islands such as Naxos and Chios traded marble and statues, such as this one, with the mainland.

Business as usual

From being a land of separate small communities, by 600 BC Greece again became a busy trading area. City traded with city, island with island. They traded in building materials, furniture, cloth, food and drink. Fine new harbours were built, on Samos for instance, and at Piraeus, the port for Athens. Many islands and cities had their specialities. For example, the island of Cos was famous for its fine fabrics.

drachma: In modern Greece money is still counted in drachmas, a word which comes from the ancient Greek *drakh*, meaning 'grasp'. Drachma meant a handful – probably of 6 bits of iron.

Athens, the business centre

Athens was the busiest city for Greek trade. It had special markets for wine, olive oil, and cheese, for tanners of leather, honey-sellers, makers of bedding and couches. And there were areas for potters' and bronze-casters' shops. There was even a 'Thieves' Harbour' near Piraeus where shady or illegal trade took place.

7th-century BC tablet showing a potter working at his wheel.

■■■LEGACY■■■

Visitors to Greece today can buy many things that were sold in the 5th century BC: olives and olive oil from Attica or Kalamata, wine from Thasos or Cephalonia, cheeses, Greek honey, beautiful fabrics and laces, small pots of perfumed oil, and so on. In Athens many of these items can be bought on Odos Pandrosou (shown above) and Odos Hephaestou – two streets in a warren of lanes and passages that have been part of the same market areas for 2000 years.

Bankers

Bankers did their business in Athens, too. Money was only invented in the 6th century BC (in Lydia). Using money, rather than doing exchanges, made trade and banking easier. That said, each city in Greece had their own style of coins so money changers and bankers needed to sort it all out.

A stamp for minting an Athenian coin. It shows the owl sacred to Athena.

One important kind of banking was lending to merchants, to hire ships and buy cargoes. Merchants paid high rates of interest, especially if the ship was to sail where pirates were busy. Unscrupulous merchants sometimes took their money and vanished. Many ships sank 'accidentally'.

A 4th-century BC four-drachma coin from the colony of Ephesos (on the coast of modern Turkey). The bee was the symbol of Ephesos.

IMPORTS AND EXPORTS

Merchants carried goods from the rich Greek cities to countries outside the Greek world. They sailed to Egypt, Macedonia and Thrace, to Italy and the lands round the Black Sea.

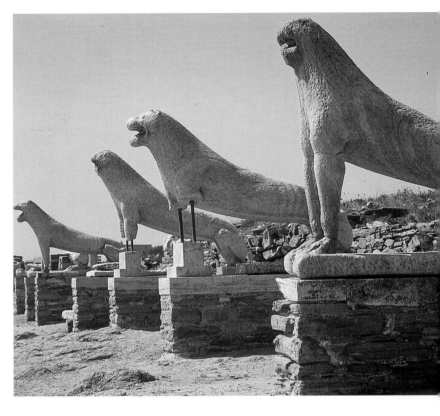

Lions of Naxos marble guard the Sacred Way on Delos, the island sacred to Apollo. The lions show an Egyptian influence, probably resulting from trading contacts.

In the 7th century BC, Corinth exported speciality perfume containers, like this owl-shaped one.

Selling and buying

These countries wanted many things from Greece: olive oil, wine, silver, pottery, sculpture, furniture, clothing and books. On the return journeys merchant ships brought things the Greeks didn't produce enough of themselves: timber from Macedonia, corn from the Black Sea, and various luxury items. Slaves could be sold at a good price in the Greek homeland. From the east came perfume and spices, from Egypt wheat, linen, papyrus and precious things.

Wheat

Many Greek cities did not grow enough wheat. Athens always needed grain. It came at first from Egypt and Sicily, then from the Black Sea. For long periods, the Athenians controlled the grain route from the Black Sea. They built military fortresses on its northern coast, and collected a 10 per cent toll on ships passing through the narrow Hellespont channel that joined the Black Sea to the Aegean. In wartime escort ships guarded the grain ships.

Wine was another Greek export. This 6th-century BC vase shows the grape harvest.

bible: One product that the Greeks sent abroad was books. The word 'bible', which we use to describe a big authoritative book or the sacred writings of Christianity, The Bible, comes from the Greek word for book, *biblion*.

A weapon of war

Sparta, often Athens' enemy, usually had plenty of wheat. It came from Messenia, the country farmed by Sparta's semi-slave — *helot* — population. It was a great advantage in wartime; cities won wars by cutting off the enemy's food supply. Timber, which by the 6th century BC was also scarce in Greece, was an important import and, like wheat, the trade became a weapon in war.

Greek olive groves produced vast amounts of olives and olive oil for export. They still do today.

QUARRELSOME GREEKS

Greek wars were not like modern wars, widely spread and continuous. Even long wars were mainly on-and-off struggles, and most were soon over. But war was an important part of Greek life, and most Greek men could expect to be involved in a war at some time or other.

A soldier leaving for war has shaken hands with his father and faces his mother.

In times of war, the people of Corinth retreated to their high fortified acropolis.

kudos: This word has come straight from Greek into English. In Greek it meant fame or glory, usually achieved in battle, whilst in English we use it to mean the credit you earn when you've done something well – 'brownie points'.

The causes of war

Greeks went to war for different reasons. They invaded the lands of native peoples in Africa, Asia and Europe – for land, slaves, precious metals and trade. They fought to defend Greece against invaders. And they regularly fought each other, city against city, often to keep control of a trade – in timber, wheat or metals. Then when Athens was very powerful, there were wars between her and the cities that revolted against her control.

Agricultural land

Many quarrels between neighbouring city-states were about farmland, and because farmer-soldiers didn't want to guard distant borders, or spend much time fighting, disputes were settled by arranged battles, usually on flat land not used for farming. They often tried to have a fighting season after the harvest.

A 6th-century BC vase picture of two warriors fighting.

Sparta

For most citizen soldiers war interrupted work. In Sparta it was different. Spartan citizens were not allowed to work. They were permanently ready for battle. From the age of seven boys lived away from home, 'boarding' in military-style schools, and men spent more time in barracks rather than at home. The Spartans' farming was done for them by Messenian *helots*, who had lost their freedom to Sparta in a war.

A 6th-century BC bronze figure of a Spartan soldier.

THEIR OWN WORDS

It was a disgrace for a Spartan soldier to lose his shield (that is, run away from battle):
'Come home with your shield — or on it,' one tough Spartan mum is supposed to have said to her departing soldier son.

A Spartan poet says,
'He who falls in the front of the line and loses his life brings honour to his city, his family and his father.'

WAR ON LAND

In most states, it was Greek citizens in the assembly who decided on a war, and citizens who fought in it, together on foot, with their own armour and supplies.

Hoplites

The armour of these citizen-soldiers — hoplites — was bulky and heavy. It consisted of a long spear, a short sword, a wooden shield with a bronze rim, a bronze helmet, bronze body-protector and leg-guards. It all came to about half the weight of a man, so one of the hoplite's slaves usually carried it — with their rations — to the battle-ground. The armour was expensive and each soldier bought his own, so hoplite soldiers were mainly well-off citizens, often farmers.

A 500-BC bronze helmet. It would probably have had a crest of dyed horse hair.

A running hoplite carrying his helmet and armour.

THEIR OWN WORDS

Herodotus describes an unusual hoplite tactic that the Spartans used against the Persians:

'The Spartans had a brilliant idea... They all turned their backs and ran, pretending to be running for their lives. The Persians charged, screaming and banging their shields, but just as the gap closed the Spartans turned to face them and dealt them terrible havoc.'

20

Fighting in formation

Infantry in Greek armies fought in a phalanx — a densely-packed square that attacked at a running trot. The thud when one phalanx trundled and crunched into another must have been audible on mountain-tops. Then came the terrible push. If the first rank fell, the second took over, walking over the dead. But because Greek wars were not continuous and hoplite battles were restricted, casualties were not as high as in modern wars.

The densely-packed phalanx was very effective. At the Battle of Marathon in 490 BC, 6,400 Persians were killed and only 192 Athenians.

A Greek archer — in this case, the hero Odysseus.

Lightly-armed troops

Most armies had javelin-throwers, archers, sling-throwers and other lightly-armed troops, mostly poor peasants and shop-keepers who couldn't afford hoplite arms. They could be valuable. In one battle the Athenians were beaten by javelin-throwers. In the 5th century BC, battles between Athens and Sparta and their allies used battalions of several hundred archers, slingers and javelin-throwers.

Sparta used its *helots* as bodyguards for the Spartan soldiers. At the battle of Plataea in 479 BC, seven *helots* fought around each Spartan. This made Spartan armies almost invincible.

21

WAR at SEA

At the time of Homer's story, *The Iliad*, ships were used to transport the soldiers to Troy. Though the oarsmen were soldiers, early 'warships' were not for fighting in, or for fighting other ships.

navy: We call a collection of ships belonging to a country and the people working for them a 'navy'. 'Navy', 'naval' and 'nautical' come from the Latin *navis*, which comes from the Greek *navs* or *naos*, meaning a ship.

A changing role

After about 700 BC, ships sometimes left harbour to stop enemy ships reaching land. There were fights at sea between ships, and ships started to carry foot-soldiers for boarding or defence. The 50-oar boats of earlier times were replaced by boats with two or three banks of oars. The *trireme*, with three banks of up to 50 oars, became the favourite Greek warship. It was quick and manoeuvrable, and oarsmen could fight if necessary, but the boat also carried 60 professional soldiers.

A 6th-century vase fragment of a fast warship under sail, flanked by two more.

Pointed boar's-head ram, often made of bronze

Look out and stroke

Oarsmen, low to waterline

Mast and sail

Helmsman in high swan's-neck stern

Steering oars

A terracotta model of a warship with shields along its side.

Fighting ships

By the mid-6th century BC, sea power was a major part of warfare. Ships of war were slender and shallow-drafted, designed for speed. They improved a crucial new weapon, a metal-tipped wooden ramming spike, jutting forward from the ship just below the water-line. Real Greek sea battles started when boats started to use this fearsome weapon, giving up boarding in favour of ramming.

To avoid getting stuck, a ship rammed either the narrow stern or prow of the enemy's boat side-on, driving straight through and out the other side, shearing off a piece of ship.

PERSIAN INVADERS

From the 7th century BC, a great Persian empire grew up to the east of the Greeks. After about 550 BC, the Greek cities along the coast of Asia came under Persian rule. But the Persians wanted more territory and power over trade.

Advancing into Greece

Then in 491 BC, the Persian emperor, Darius, invaded Greece with about 100,000 troops and 300 to 600 ships. He conquered Thrace and Macedonia and then, in 490 BC, his army landed in Attica. Athens sent for help to Sparta, but the Spartans didn't arrive on time. Although the Athenians were outnumbered, they defeated the Persians at Marathon. There were 192 Athenians killed, to 6,400 Persians.

A Persian archer, part of the Royal Guard.

The Athenian Treasury at Delphi contained their spoils from the Battle of Marathon.

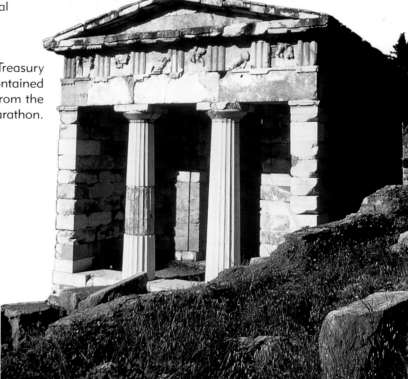

barbarian: The Greeks called anyone who didn't speak Greek *barbarikos*, because they heard a meaningless noise — a bar, bar, bar, — when foreigners spoke. That became our word 'barbarian', a wild person.

Thermopylae

The second invasion was in 480 BC, under Darius' son Xerxes. At Thermopylae, a local farmer showed the Persians a track leading from the sea up behind the mountains. When Leonidas, the Spartan king who led the Greeks, heard about this treachery, he sent all the other Greeks home, and with 300 Spartans fought to the last man without any hope of winning. Xerxes marched on into Attica. The Athenians retreated to the island of Salamis, while the Persians burnt down Athens.

A Greek hoplite (on the right) fights a Persian soldier (left).

The Battle of Salamis

But the same year at Salamis, the Persian fleet was lured towards a narrow bay. The Greek ships drove out into them, splintering their sides or sheering off ranks of Persian oars. Then they ploughed into the next wave of reinforcements. The Persians lost 200 ships, the Greeks only 40. A year later, at Plataea, the Persians were beaten on land as well.

Later, Persians fought Greeks in the Aegean, and gave money to Sparta to stir up trouble for Athens, but they did not invade the mainland again. Greece was never to be part of the great Persian Empire.

BLACK SEA

CASPIAN SEA

• Athens

• Nineveh

MEDITERRANEAN SEA

Babylon •

• Persepolis

PERSIAN GULF

PERSIAN EMPIRE

Map showing the Persian Empire at its greatest extent.

WAR INSIDE GREECE

After the Persian invasions, Athens formed an alliance of states – 'The Federation of Delos' – for defence if the Persians came again. But it was in effect an empire, with Athens as its leader collecting tribute-money.

Resentment of Athens

Many cities, especially Sparta, resented Athens' growing power. Sparta formed its own league, so that Greece was split into two camps. In 431 BC, nearly 50 years after leading the Greeks against Persia, Sparta began a war with Athens and her allies that lasted 27 years.

A bust of the Athenian leader Pericles.

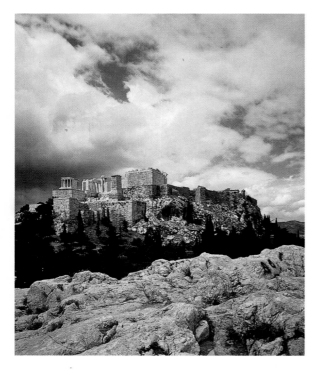

Many of the buildings of the Athenian Acropolis were built with tribute money.

Athens had a great fleet, Sparta a very powerful army. They avoided each other. The Athenian leader, Pericles, let the Spartans take over Attica and its farmland, while the Athenians stayed safe inside Athens. To maintain supplies, Pericles had defences (known as the 'Long Walls') built between Athens and Piraeus. But plague came to the city and a quarter of population died, including Pericles and two of his son

War becomes brutal

Under the next Athenian leader, Cleon, the war became brutal. When Melos rebelled against Athens, the Athenians killed the men and made slaves of the women and children. When the Spartans captured Plataea in 427 BC, they slaughtered anyone who could not prove they had been on Sparta's side.

A soldier straps on his sword. His shield and helmet lie ready.

■■■LEGACY■■■

British warships in the Atlantic guarding grain-ships, 1940.

The Second World War (1939-45) was like the Athens-Sparta conflict in some ways. Athens was in a similar position to Britain, depending for its supplies on food carried in ships. Their small convoys had escort-ships, just like the wartime food convoys that crossed the Atlantic to Britain, guarded by destroyers. By 405 BC, Sparta's navy had become stronger; Athens surrendered when it could not get its food convoys through. In the Second World War, Germany's navy became weaker, and Britain survived.

Fighting at sea

For most of the war Athenian ships kept the grain routes from the Black Sea safe. But more and more of Athens' allies broke away. In the end, Athens was fighting to protect its grain route.

In the last years of the war Sparta was helped by Persian money. They built their own fleet and in 405 BC, won a victory at sea. After that, Athens could not protect its grain-ships. So in the winter of 404 BC, its citizens starving, Athens was forced to surrender.

PHILIP AND ALEXANDER

In the 4th century BC, Greece slowly weakened itself with more wars. Something needed to be done. Two great Greek leaders, father and son, worked to make Greece strong again.

Philip II

Between 357 and 336 BC, Philip II, King of Macedon, Thebes and Athens, gradually overpowered all of Greece with his huge armies. Philip had full-time soldiers. He thought up new tactics and tougher training. Philip planned to invade Persia, to punish them, he said, for Darius' invasion 150 years before. He probably had his eye on the gold and riches of Asia too. But after announcing his plan he was murdered.

A gold medallion showing Philip II of Macedonia, conqueror of Greece.

Alexander the Great

Philip II's son, Alexander, inherited a united Greece from his father. He took over the army, and crossed into Asia. He craved fame, but also had enormous debts to pay off. He needed the wealth of Asia and to control its trading links. Marching south, Alexander won many battles.

In a mosaic from Pompeii, Italy, Alexander fights the Persians at the Battle of Issus, 333 BC.

Thousands of paid soldiers created widespread destruction, sometimes of whole cities. Bigger warships and new inventions — like siege catapults and moveable towers — were used. Alexander defeated Darius, the Persian Emperor, and took his gold. He marched on to modern Afghanistan, into India and back along the Persian Gulf. He covered amazing distances with a huge army and cavalry. Alexander died in Babylon in 323 BC, aged 32, but he left an extraordinary legacy behind.

catapult: Our word is from the Greek word *katapeltis*, made by combining *kata*, against, and *peltis* a shield. Perhaps the Greek catapult was designed especially to damage shields.

Map showing the extent of Alexander's empire and the route of his armies.

⬛ ALEXANDER'S EMPIRE
➡ ROUTE OF HIS ARMY

A new Greek world

Everywhere he went Alexander founded cities, laying them out in a Greek grid plan, with Greek buildings like theatres and *gymnasia*. To this new world, the Greeks took all their learning, arts and technology. The silk-route from China led directly into the Greek-Indian kingdom of Bactria. Scents and spices, gold and luxury goods poured in. From trade and warfare, a new Greek civilization, known as the Hellenistic, was born — an extraordinary mixture of European, African and Asiatic cultures.

Alexander sculpted to resemble a god. He encouraged people to worship and adore him like a god.

29

GLOSSARY

Afghanistan: the country lying between modern Iran and Pakistan.

alabaster: an attractive hard white rock that can be carved into objects, such as lamps or boxes.

Aristotle (384-322 BC): a famous philosopher and writer. He wrote about many things, including politics, science and how people behave. He thought men naturally fought, plundered, and 'hunted' each other.

Babylon: Major city and centre of power in the ancient world located on the River Euphrates, in what is now Iraq.

Bactria: an ancient kingdom in the north of modern Afghanistan.

bronze: a metal alloy (blend) of mainly copper with some tin to strengthen it.

city-state: a small state that included a city at its centre and the surrounding countryside and villages. From about 800 to 400 BC, Greece was divided into a series of city-states, each with their own laws, systems of government and coinage.

Cleon (died 422 BC): ruler of Athens after Pericles, The son of a wealthy tanner, his policies led to Athens' defeat by Sparta.

colony: a settlement of people who have left their own homes to live somewhere else. After about 800 BC, Greek cities sent out many colonists.

Darius (reigned 522-486 BC): the emperor of Persia (Achaemenid dynasty) who invaded Greece in 491.

gymnasion: a sports centre with all kinds of equipment and facilities for track and field events. Wherever they went the Greeks built gymnasia.

helot: a slave from Messenia, who served the Spartans, giving them farm produce, manual labour and military service.

Herodotus (c. 480-425 BC): sometimes called the first historian, Herodotus wrote about the wars between the Greeks and Persians. He travelled all over the Greek world, collecting information about different peoples and customs.

TIMELINE

c. 8000 BC	Early trade across Aegean, e.g. in flint.	c. 800	Greeks trading from Al Mina, Syria, North Africa and Egypt.	735	First Sicilian colony, Naxos.
c. 3000	Greek bronze being made.			733	Corkyra and Syracuse founded by Corinth.
c. 1500	Mycenaeans trading.	c. 800-500	Greeks settling all round Mediterranean and Black Sea.	730-710	Spartans conquer and enslave Messenians.
c. 1200	Mycenaean palaces burnt.				
c. 1100	Greeks begin to migrate to coast of Asia (modern Turkey) – 'Ionian' Greece.	776	Traditional date for first all-Greece Olympic Games.	c. 700	Athens combines with towns of Attica to make one city-state.
c. 1050	Iron being used for weapons and tools.	c. 750-700	Homer composes his poems.	c. 700	Poet Hesiod composing.
		c. 750	Greeks borrow and adapt Phoenician alphabet.	630	Cyrene founded in Africa.
c. 1000-750	Phoenicians prosperous, travelling and trading.			c. 600	Founding of Massalia.
c. 900-750	Trade in 'geometric' vases.	750 on	Heavy hoplite armour being used.	c. 600	First battles at sea.

Homer (c. 8th century BC): the blind poet who composed two great story-poems, *The Iliad* and *The Odyssey*, about the Greeks' war with the Trojans, and their return home.

hoplite: a heavily-armed foot-soldier, who fought with other hoplites in a tight phalanx.

Lydia: a large civilized country lying behind the coastal Greek settlements in Ionia (part of modern Turkey). Its king was Croesus.

Magna Graecia: 'Great Greece' was the name given to the part of Sicily and southern Italy colonized by Greeks.

ore: the raw material for a metal. For instance, iron ore is mined and iron extracted from it.

Peloponnese: the large area of land in the south of Greece, below the Gulf of Corinth.

Pericles (c. 495-429 BC): leader of Athens from about 454 to 429. He was responsible for the rebuilding of Athens after the Persian invasion.

Persian Empire: the empire with its centre in modern Iran, which invaded Greece in the 5th century BC. Also known as the Achaemenid Empire, after its ruling family.

phalanx: a square fight formation made up of rows of hoplite soldiers.

Phoenicians: people from the eastern Mediterranean (modern Lebanon and part of Syria) who were successful traders and travellers from about 1050 BC onwards.

Sparta: the chief city-state of the Peloponnese, in southern Greece, and often Athens' rival and enemy. Sparta was famed for its obsession with war, and the tough way it brought up children.

Thucydides (c. 455-400 BC): a general in the Athenian army, who wrote a famous history of the war between Athens and Sparta and their allies. The war was later called the 'Peloponnesian War'.

Trireme: ship with three rows of oarsmen. Each row sat on benches at different levels, using oars of different lengths. A *trireme* might have 150 oarsmen.

Xerxes (reigned 486-465 BC): a Persian king, the son of Darius. Xerxes invaded Greece in 480.

after 600	Coins begin to circulate.
545	Persia conquers Ionians.
493	Rich strike of silver at Laurium in Attica, pays for warships to be built.
491	First Persian invasion, under Darius – Greek victory at Marathon.
480	Second Persian invasion, under Xerxes – Greeks beaten at Thermopylae. Athens burnt by Persians, Greeks win at Salamis.
479	Greeks win at Platea, Persians go home.
461	Pericles leader in Athens.
449	Peace of Callias – wars with Persia officially ended.
c.445-426	Herodotus writing.
431-404	War between Athens and Sparta (Peloponnesian War).
431	Thucydides starts writing.
429	Pericles dies of plague.
425	Athenians beat Spartans at Pylos – Spartan offer of peace refused by Cleon.
425	Aristophanes' first anti-war play produced.
404	Athens surrenders to Sparta.
357-336	Philip II of Macedon extends power over all mainland Greece.
336	Death of Philip.
334	Alexander crosses into Asia.
333-324	Alexander's victorious campaigns in Egypt, Persia, India.
323	Death of Alexander.

INDEX